the Bulldog

By Sarah Voss

Illustrated by Carolyn Paplham

Dedicated to Bella who inspired me to write this;
Jonah who inspired me to finish it;
and Ryan, who encouraged and supported me from the beginning and always.

Luna Regular (title font) was created by Amanda Leeson

Bully dog, Bully dog, Bella, Bella the bully dog.

B the bully dog.

She runs like a cheetah.

Has stripes like a tiger.

Has the ears of a rabbit.

Eats like a mammoth.

Snores like a bear.

Hops like a kangaroo.

Roars like a dinosaur.

Stretches like a cat.

Yawns like
a lion.

Burrows like a gopher.

Roams like a panther.

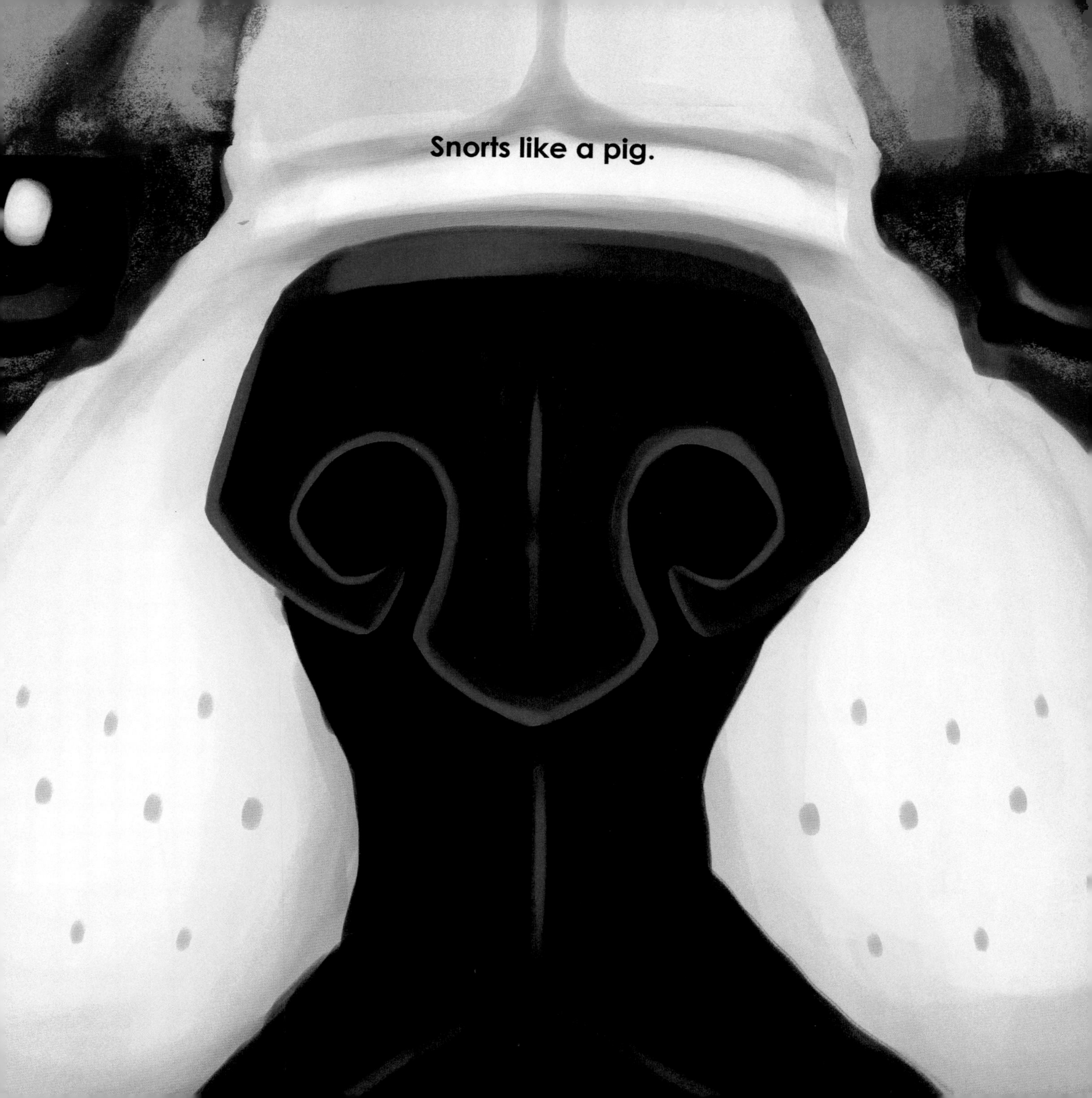

Snorts like a pig.

Has the teeth of a shark.

Howls like a wolf.

Has the eyes of an owl.

Has the tummy
of a cow.

Feels free as a bird.

But Bella IS a bulldog. A friendly bully dog.

And the best cheetah, tiger, rabbit, mammoth, bear, kangaroo, dinosaur, cat, lion, gopher, panther, pig, shark, wolf, owl, cow, bird... BULLDOG!

And now Lola wants a book about her...
(if you know Lola, this comes as no surprise!)

Made in the USA
Coppell, TX
08 December 2019